D1505467

PRAISE FOR *The* **BUCKET LIST** *Book*

"Please don't have a midlife crisis. But if you do, drop everything and read this book. It will not only change the way you think about your life, but how you choose to live it. And the good news is that you end up smiling!"

—Richard Leider, international-bestselling author of *The Power of Purpose*, *Repacking Your Bags*, and *Life Reimagined*

"I couldn't put it down—a fun read! It helped me to revisit and rebuild my Bucket List, to dream more, and learn more—and it gave me the tools to do more."

—Brad Lantz, business mentor

"What an outstanding read! This book showed me that a Bucket List is more than a tool to describe my wild and crazy adventure dreams. It's a place to sketch out my leadership aspirations, life goals, AND adventures . . . and will serve as the motivation I need to achieve them. Chapter 7 on aspirational leadership and a Bucket List is a must read for all leaders seeking to bring out the best in others."

—Jennifer Myster, president, Allina Health–Buffalo

"Inspiring! Very positive and uplifting read. *The Bucket List Book* made me realize life can be so rich when we challenge ourselves to reach our goals and make checks off our Bucket List."

—Bill Lunn, Emmy-winning anchor/reporter
and author of *Heart of a Ranger*

"This book reminds us that creating (and sharing) our Bucket List is a great way to encourage aspiration—instead of stagnation—in both our professional and personal lives."

—John Hallberg, CEO,
Children's Cancer Research Fund

"Paul's done it again—taken a very simple concept and made it come alive for me as a leader. Every good leader needs a Bucket List, and this book will make that process fun!"

—Dan Mallin, cofounder, Minnesota Cup,
Magnet 360, and Equals 3

"This is a great little book! It's very thought provoking and inspiring. Paul gives us a good poke in the ribs to get out of our comfort zones and do something exciting with our lives."

—Jeff Given, president, Bercom

"I love this book! It's simple, it's fun, it's inspiring, and it reminded me there are so many things I want to do!"

—Dave Ryan, radio personality and author of
*Take a Shower, Show Up on Time,
and Don't Steal Anything*

"Wherever you are on your aspirational journey, this is the book for you!"

—Lynn Casey, chair & CEO, Padilla

"Reading *The Bucket List Book* was a transforming experience, and it took me less than two hours! Previously, I had always considered a Bucket List as something for the later years in life. . . . Now, I see my Bucket List as something to be lived out in all of my years. My Bucket List begins today! I am looking forward to someday saying 'I'm glad we did' instead of 'I wish we had . . .'"

—John Gamades, partner at OrangeBall Creative

the BUCKET LIST *Book*

How *Aspirational* Thinking Improves Life and Leadership

Foreword by Kevin Warren, COO, Minnesota Vikings

Includes Research, Worksheets & the Game

HANDy Paint Pail
Painting just got easier!®

TRY ME!

Paul Batz *with* Mark Bergman

Hardcover ISBN 13: 978-1-63489-051-9
Paperback ISBN: 978-1-63489-061-8
e-book ISBN: 978-1-63489-052-6
Library of Congress Number: 2017937590

Printed in the United States of America
First Printing: 2017

21 20 19 18 17   5 4 3 2 1

Cover and interior design by James Monroe Design, LLC.

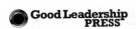

Wise Ink, Inc.
837 Glenwood Avenue, Minneapolis, Minnesota, 55405
wiseinkpub.com
To order, visit goodleadership.com
Reseller discounts available.

Good Leadership PRESS

About Good Leadership Press

Good Leadership Press publishes exciting little books on positive leadership that can be read in less than two hours. The books feature stories of goodness at work in the world, with practical leadership strategies and coaching tools for increasing personal growth.

Goodness Pays

One dollar from each of the first 5,000 copies sold of each book published under the Good Leadership Press imprint will benefit a charity that ties to the book's theme. *The Bucket List Book* will benefit the Make-A-Wish Foundation.

Goodness pays, because goodness grows!
To learn more about Good Leadership Press, visit goodleadership.com.

Dedication

Special thanks to Delane, Carolyn, and Linda, who said many times: "This book is begging to be written!" We proceeded, inspired by this quote, from the author of *The Alchemist*, Paulo Coelho: *"It's the possibility of having a dream come true that makes life interesting."* We agree.

Contents

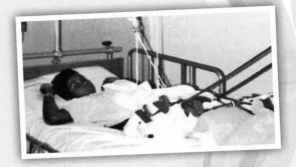

Kevin Warren, 1976, age twelve

Kevin Warren, today

FOREWORD

When you spend months in a full-body cast as a twelve-year-old, you have lots of time to think.

I was hit by a car in 1976 and flew almost thirty feet. In the ambulance on the way to the hospital, the EMTs freely speculated that I wouldn't survive—until one woman said, "Don't say that." She looked at me and said, "You are going to make it, and you are going to have a good life."

I realized then that the nurse was trying to help me think positively about my dire situation. And her words had an impact beyond that moment; she helped me be optimistic about my future throughout the coming months, when I could have easily spiraled into pure negativity.

I spent many weeks in a hospital bed in traction and many months in my bed at home wearing a full-body cast. With no cable television or Internet, I would lie there with only my bedpan and my thoughts. I imagined who I was going to be and what I was going to do when I got out of that room. I knew that when I got my cast off, I would struggle to walk ten feet—but I still dreamed of running a mile, playing college sports, and having a great life. Little did I know, I was starting my Bucket List.

Forty years later, I have a fuller life than I ever dreamed. I was a Division I basketball player and was inducted into the Grand Canyon University Athletics Hall of Fame in 2012. I graduated from Arizona State University's MBA program and Notre Dame Law School, and today I am the highest-ranking African American business-side executive in the National Football League. I have been married to the same woman for twenty-five years, and we have been blessed with two healthy and talented children. My wife, Greta, and I agreed to donate one million dollars to the University of Minnesota Masonic Children's Hospital for pediatric care in honor of my late sister. The aspirational thinking that I started at age twelve—my Bucket List—launched the entire course of my life.

The aspirational thinking that I started at age twelve—my Bucket List—launched the entire course of my life.

Paul Batz has been my executive coach since 2013. As I made the leap from lawyer to leader, Paul reminded me that if I wanted to be a leader, I could not simply rely on my lawyer expertise; I also had to bring vision alive through the people around me. Paul told me, "You know, you are not done living your Bucket List. You will become a good leader when you start helping others live their Bucket Lists also."

Paul was exactly right; I am not done with my Bucket List. I still want to hug my future grandkids, live to be one hundred years old, donate one million dollars a year to charitable causes, and of course, win a Super Bowl with the Vikings!

I am convinced that everyone should have a Bucket List. A Bucket List is personal and ever-changing—something to be cherished and shared. Maybe it will help you focus on saving money, planning for the future, or asking for help. Maybe it will help propel you to huge achievements. My Bucket List gave me a reason to live. I hope building your Bucket List has an impact on you—because the way you think can save your life.

KEVIN WARREN, COO OF THE
MINNESOTA VIKINGS, NFL

Mark Bergman

INTRODUCTION

By Mark Bergman, CEO
HANDy Paint Products

I should probably explain why there's a picture of a HANDy Paint Pail on the cover of this book. Fifteen years ago, I invented the HANDy Paint Pail, and today it's one of the most successful patents in the painting industry. At Good Leadership Enterprises's monthly Good Leadership Breakfasts, Paul Batz has a different name for it: the "Bucket of Goodwill." Together, we use the Bucket of Goodwill to raise money for charity, and over six years, we've raised over $200,000 for organizations around the country. Neither Paul nor I could ever have guessed that my little invention would become such a symbol of goodness and giving.

In this book, the bucket doesn't only signify generosity—it's also our representation of a Bucket List. I took risks and embraced aspirational thinking to accomplish one of my Bucket List goals, which was to invent an industry-changing patent. Aspirational thinking helped me make my dreams a reality, and I hope this book guides you toward your own dreams.

The first step to living your dreams is filling your Bucket List with your greatest aspirations—because if you're not dreaming it, you're not making progress!

What are you putting in your bucket?

—Mark Bergman, CEO, HANDy Paint Products.

CHAPTER 1:

What Is a Bucket List?

By Paul Batz, CEO
Good Leadership Enterprises

What is a Bucket List? Maybe that's a silly question. We all *know* what a Bucket List is . . .

In doing the research for this book, even the college interns on our Good Leadership Enterprises team were aware of the term *Bucket List*. However, I was surprised to learn the term is relatively new: the first mention in traditional media was in 2004 by author Patrick M. Carlisle to describe a list of things you want to do before you die—or, "kick the bucket." The phrase *kick the bucket* is much older, used since the late eighteenth century.

The term *Bucket List* was in the 2007 movie of the same name starring Morgan Freeman and Jack Nicholson. The two men in the film are dying, and their unlikely friendship pushes them to accomplish items on their Bucket Lists, including international travel, fine dining, and reconnecting with family.

Because of that movie, it's easy to assume a Bucket List has to do with dying. But it doesn't.

This book is about what a Bucket List has to do with living.

This book is about what a Bucket List has to do with living.

We all can benefit from a Bucket List. Without clear, positive goals, it's easy to get stuck in the mundane routines of life—going through the motions without dreaming about our futures. Sure, you might think about the next *step*: your next promotion, your kid's next school year, your next car. But it takes a lot more work to dream about the next *level*, much less make that dream a reality.

Let me be clear: When I say we can all benefit from a Bucket List, I don't mean those loosely defined goals forming like clouds in the back of our minds. I mean a piece of paper with aspirations written down. Lofty or modest, the first step to reaching something you want is giving it a name. The second step is writing it down on paper. Then, the best opportunity for enjoying your Bucket List is involved in answering three questions: What is it? When do you want it? Who do you want to help you? More on those three steps later.

The First Bucket List Research Project

The premise of this book rests on my experience as a business owner and executive coach and on empirical data collected by Jeri Meola, the CEO of SMS Research, headquartered in Minneapolis, Minnesota. She and I are fascinated by the magnetism of people who live aspirational lives. Our first instinct was to scan the Internet for existing research; imagine our surprise when we found nothing. Nearly every reference to "Bucket List" has to do with gift items, or PR firm–generated suggestions of what people "should have" on their Bucket List.

So Jeri, Mark Bergman, and I decided to do the first research project of its kind on the Bucket List.

Four hundred people living in the United States were randomly selected to participate using an online national panel. They were told my firm, Good Leadership Enterprises, sponsored the research, and they had only two days in November of 2016 to complete the survey.

We asked about:

- Attitudes toward their Bucket Lists
- Their number-one items
- What was most important
- How they created their lists
- How often they modify or update their lists
- Whether they have completion dates associated with the items
- Whether they have their lists written down

Jeri shared her excitement about the results of the research. "The majority of people, regardless of their age, see a Bucket List as an aspirational concept that ensures they live a fulfilling life NOW," she said. "It's no surprise the number-one item for most people is about travel, but I do find it fascinating so many people say their Bucket List helps keep them focused on career goals."

Research Notes: The data from the Bucket List survey has a statistical accuracy of plus or minus 5.0 percent.

I interviewed Jeri to find out how my thoughts fit with the research:

So, Jeri, are men and women equally likely to have a Bucket List?

Yes! In our random survey, 51 percent of the four hundred people were female, and 49 percent were male.

Women are more likely to buy something they never dreamed of, and it's more important that their Bucket Lists expresses gratitude as an expression of their faith and leads to a life of hope.

The men who have Bucket Lists are older than the women who have Bucket Lists, and it is more important to them that their Bucket Lists are related to achieving a career goal or leaving a legacy.

Are older people more likely to have a Bucket List?

No, not really. More than half of the people who have a Bucket List (56 percent) are between the ages of twenty-five and fifty-four, so that's more middle-aged than younger or older. Fourteen percent are under the age of twenty-four, and only seventeen percent are over the age of sixty-five.

What is the most likely predictor of whether or not someone will have a Bucket List?

We learned 73 percent of people who have a Bucket List have at least some college education. Those in that group say their Bucket List helps keep them focused on career goals. They are also more likely to keep their Bucket List private.

Were there any patterns for the types of items people have on their Bucket List?

Yes. The items can be categorized into four general themes: Travel, Treasures, Experiences, and Accomplishments.

The most frequent number-one item for a Bucket List is about **Travel***; 35 percent say they have an item to "visit a country, city, or famous landmark." And if your number-one item is "visit a new country," you are more likely to review your Bucket List every time a vacation comes up.*

Treasures *include keepsakes, tools for hobbies, or collections that bring us joy. Examples we found include buying a boat, special car, musical instrument, special piece of artwork, or a rare base-ball card.*

51%
Women

49%
Men

56%
25 and 54

14% Under 24

17% Over 65

Experiences *include adventures, which bring extra meaning, thrills, or fun to life. Some examples we found include volunteering and helping people, being philanthropic, creating family memories, and attending rare or exclusive events like the Olympics.*

Accomplishments *include goals or endeavors signified by a commitment over time to achieve. Examples we found include writing a book; learning a new life skill such as a language, sport, or musical instrument; donating a specific amount of money; building a house; buying a farm; or selling a business.*

The Bucket List items of most importance were about family, personal health, and having fun. That means doing things with others, staying positive, and being independent in how we live.

I'm curious—is creating a Bucket List a private or a collaborative exercise?

We learned that 83 percent of people say they "did it by themselves"; 12 percent said they created their list with a spouse; and the other 5 percent created the list with friends, family, parents, grandparents, and coworkers.

Do you have any idea whether or not most Bucket Lists are more likely to be informal (unwritten) or formally written down?

I found it interesting that more people have informal or unwritten Bucket Lists—especially because so many people use their Bucket Lists to help ensure career goals. The data says that 54 percent of people have their Bucket List in their memory while 46 percent have them written. If you have the Bucket List items in your memory, you are less likely to think you will accomplish the items. If you have

Ideas for My Bucket List

_____

_____

_____

_____

_____

_____

_____

grandchildren, you are the most likely to have your Bucket List written.

People who have grandchildren see a Bucket List as being important for:

1. Keeping from being stuck in life
2. Staying aspirational rather than practical
3. Maintaining a healthy spiritual life
4. Being intentional about family
5. Having more aspirations met

Were you able to identify the main benefits of a written Bucket List?

Here's what the people with written Bucket Lists shared about the benefits that were different from the benefits seen by people whose Bucket Lists were not written.

The written Bucket List:

1. Helps to keep focus on personal goals
2. Keeps people from being "stuck" at any time in life
3. Helps to have a better life

The Bucket List items of most importance were about family, personal health, and having fun.

83%
Created Their Bucket List by Themselves

12% with a Spouse

5% Other

4. Increases confidence in completing important
items

So, if a Bucket List is a living document, how frequently are they updated?

*Over 50 percent of the respondents are actively
involved and update their Bucket List more than one
time per year; 36 percent change their Bucket List
yearly, 13 percent say they update it monthly, and
7 percent say they update weekly and daily. That
also means 29 percent of people say they have not
changed the items on their Bucket List.*

Did you learn anything about the length of time people give themselves to accomplish items on their Bucket List?

*It's particularly interesting to me that 84 percent of
the items on Bucket Lists have no firm completion
date—a wide-open time frame only limited by their
creator's own life span.*

*For those with time frames attached, ten years is the
most common time frame for completing items on
a Bucket List. And with that data, we also learned
most people have completed 25 percent of the items
on their Bucket Lists. And 25 percent of the people*

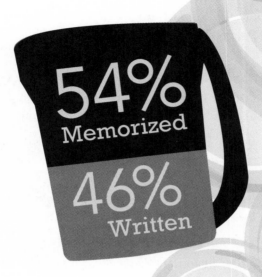

54%
Memorized

46%
Written

Ideas for My Bucket List

_____

_____

_____

_____

_____

who have Bucket Lists do not expect to complete their Bucket Lists.

You mentioned to me your fascination with the fact that most of the people who have a Bucket List prefer to keep their list private. What's that all about?

Well, if only 17 percent of people think about their Bucket List as an end-of-life activity, then that makes me even more interested in the fact that more than half of people with a Bucket List do not share their lists with other people.

Similarly, more than half say "just having a Bucket List"—sharing or not—helps them stay focused on how to have a better life, and 40 percent say having a Bucket List helps them from feeling "stuck" in their lives.

Did you specifically ask about how the Bucket List leads to a better life?

Yes, and 22 percent say their Bucket List helps articulate life goals, dreams, and adventures; 17 percent say a Bucket List is important for motivation; and 10 percent say "it makes me happy"—being happy is certainly a part of a better life. Only 7 percent say it's about accomplishing something before death.

50%+
Actively Updated
the List

29%
Never Changed
the List

84%
No Completion
Date

25%
Completed
Items

25%
Expect to
NOT Complete
the List

I am wondering if differences in personal characteristics such as income level, ethnicity, and marital status have any impact on how Bucket Lists are used or perceived. Did you consider that?

Yes, I think asking those questions about our participants is really important. We found 73 percent of the people who have Bucket Lists earn $75,000 a year or less. Also, the higher your income, the more likely the Bucket List items are aspirational rather than practical.

African Americans tend to use their Bucket Lists to help them stay focused on goals and view their lists as a moral compass. They also are more likely to have the lists written formally and review their lists more frequently. White people are more likely to set specific dates for completion of the items.

So who is most likely to have a Bucket List, and why?

Married people and people living in a marriage-like relationship are more likely to have a Bucket List than others. That group in particular believes "everyone should have a Bucket List if they want to lead a better life," and they are more likely to have completed important items on their list.

83%
List Helps Live
a Better Life

17% Important
Motivation

22%
Articulate Life
Goals

12% Motivating

10% It Makes Me Happy

7% Accomplish before Death

Single respondents are the most likely to have something challenging or adventurous, like going skydiving, bungee jumping, mountain climbing, or white-water rafting, as most important. Also, an adult living alone sees being energized and enjoying life as most important.

Finally, it's not surprising to learn empty nesters— people who have raised children who have left the home—tend to have completed the most items on their lists.

Jeri finished our conversation by revisiting the part of the research that energized her personally:

What I found interesting is that most people keep their lists private, like their dreams should be a secret . . . but the data proves that sharing a list vastly increases the likelihood that someone will accomplish their goals! I think we have a huge opportunity to let people know that sharing their Bucket List puts them on the path to crossing off the most important items. That's what makes this research, and this book, so exciting!

So, how could we close the first chapter without asking Jeri what's on her Bucket List?

Jeri's Top Five Bucket List Items:

1. Golf at a links course in Scotland

2. See the Pope conduct Easter Mass in Rome

3. Visit Barbra Streisand's home

4. Throw one-dollar bills off the Empire State Building

5. Take my family on a cruise in honor of my mother

When it comes to starting your Bucket List, think big and dream free. The magic starts when you share your Bucket List, pray, or meditate on believing in what's possible!

CHAPTER 2:

Are You Keeping Your Bucket List a Secret?

For some reason, sharing a Bucket List isn't as easy as playing the "What if I win the lottery?" game. Winning the lottery is extremely unlikely, so the brainstorming is free-flowing and safe.

The Bucket List hits closer to home.

Recently, I asked a friend over lunch about whether she would ever tell anyone what's on her Bucket List, and how she reacted was revealing:

"No, because what if I fail? What if I literally let myself down?"

Her meaning: *Sharing my Bucket List is a risk. Sharing my goals with other people opens the possibility that I will not reach my goal, which I interpret as failure. If I keep my Bucket List private, I will protect myself from myself.*

It's understandable.

And so is the person who rejects the Bucket List idea altogether. Another friend shared, "I don't have a Bucket List anymore. Recently I began studying mindfulness and meditation. I've learned to reduce my stress by focusing on the present and trying to accept everything as a gift." I understand that, too.

If you've read this far, you are at least considering the benefits of a Bucket List, and hopefully your mind is open to sharing it with others. However, I have to admit through my own experiences that sharing aspirations is not without consequences.

Recently, I discussed the premise of *The Bucket List Book* with friends at a dinner party. When I asked the question: "So what's on your Bucket List?" the room went eerily quiet. Hmmm . . .

Through further conversation, I learned there were two points of hesitation hanging in the awkward silence:

1. A Bucket List is not to be taken lightly. People really want to think about it before they speak.

2. Some people make value judgments about the items on another's Bucket List. That's what makes it risky to go too deep, too fast.

That sounds familiar. Twice in my life I was reprimanded by authority figures when I shared specific items on my Bucket List. Once, I mentioned to a supervisor that *Do something worthy of being selected to give a college commencement address* was on my Bucket List. That supervisor said to me afterward: "That sounds conceited. What's going on in your ego to cause you to desire that?" That hurt. But ten years later, when I gave the commencement address at DeVry University, it felt fantastic!

Another time, when I said out loud that I wanted to write a best-selling book, a person I respected said: "Books are dying. That's a stupid goal." Ouch again.

But more than a hundred times over, the responses I've gotten from sharing my Bucket List items have been pure goodness. I've experienced an outpouring of love and support from people who are more likely to say, "That's cool!" or "I can help you with that."

Most recently, I enjoyed my first Packers game outdoors at Lambeau Field in Green Bay. It was courtesy of a friend who heard me say: "I want to see a Green Bay Packers game in Lambeau Field" out loud while playing the Bucket List Game (Chapter 8 in this book). It turned out to be a double thrill—for me, and for the family and friends of the person who took me to the game. I commemorated the event by purchasing my own Green Bay Packers jersey with the name "Bucket List" printed on the back.

Paul Batz attended his first Green Bay Packers game at Lambeau Field in September of 2016. Thanks to Paul Hillen, who made it happen.

To Share or Not to Share

What we learned through empirical and social research is that most of us have Bucket List goals in our head . . . but most of us don't share our list with others. The resistance is rooted in fear and a desire to protect ourselves.

But here's the deal: People want to help each other. That's what a good life is all about.

There are no guarantees with a Bucket List, but there's also very little risk. You don't have to write a book on the subject, and you certainly don't have to broadcast your Bucket Lists on the same scale that I do.

The simplest way is to find a confidant—a best friend, colleague, mate, or spouse who's willing to help. By sharing each other's Bucket List, you are creating a *personal contract*, a promise to keep the dreams alive and make progress.

By sharing each other's Bucket Lists, you are creating a personal contract.

CHAPTER 3:
Aspirational Thinking

Aspirations are positive, compelling goals that bring out the best in human beings, helping us overcome our natural negativity and hard-to-break habits. Aspirations are fundamentally based in hope and built on a belief in basic human goodness.

The publishing industry bears witness to the power of aspirational, positive thinking. Aspirational books like these have sold millions and millions worldwide:

- *How to Win Friends and Influence People* by Dale Carnegie (1936)

- *Think and Grow Rich* by Napoleon Hill (1937)

- *The Power of Positive Thinking* by Norman Vincent Peale (1952)

- *The Greatest Salesman in the World* by Og Mandino (1968)

- *You Can Heal Your Life* by Louise Hay (1984)

- *You'll See It When You Believe It* by Wayne Dyer (1989)

- *The Art of Possibility* by Benjamin Zander and Rosamund Stone Zander (2002)

These and other contemporary authors like Tony Robbins and Oprah Winfrey rehash the same theme: compelling goals and positive belief systems will improve your life. But none of them explicitly use a Bucket List as a framework.

Something To Look Forward To

In casual conversation, the Bucket List idea is commonly shared in the context of dying: *What are you going to do before you kick the bucket?* is the assumption. But as we learned in our research, most people who have a Bucket List create it to enhance their living *now*.

At eighty years old, my mom uses her Bucket List to build excitement about every new day. She sees her Bucket

List as an everyday itinerary of things to look forward to—she has every reason to keep adding to the list, because her mother lived to the age of 103!

One of Mom's recent accomplishments was moving to live in the city to be closer to her grandkids. By moving from a rural lake to the big city, she opened up a whole new world of opportunities for herself in her seventies.

> *Most people who have a Bucket List create it to enhance their living **NOW**.*

Aspirations and Purpose

Bestselling author and executive coach Richard J. Leider is partnering with AARP to improve the quality of life for seniors just like my mom. In the book *Life Reimagined: Discovering Your New Life Possibilities*—which he coauthored with Allan M. Webber, cofounder of *Fast Company* magazine—Leider recommends an artful mix of both deep reflection and aspirational thinking to define purpose in life.

His work is really important because AARP studies have shown that business owners and leaders

> *Is it possible a Bucket List can literally keep us alive?*

who retire without aspirations die prematurely. Is it possible a Bucket List can literally keep us alive?

Janice Holly Booth, reporting in *AARP: The Magazine* on *Life Reimagined*, characterized a sense of purpose as "recognizing what you want out of life and having a plan to achieve it." She cited a study by a research team at Flanders University in Adelaide, Australia, who followed 1,475 adults over an eighteen-year period beginning in 1992.

They found that people with higher scoring on "sense of purpose" had better health and fewer symptoms of depression and functional disability. They also had better short-term memory and mental speed. Additionally, having a stronger sense of purpose helped people build a better buffer against the normal stress of living and aging. But more importantly, having clear goals and aspirations made it easier to cope with the unexpected stressors in a long life.

A similar study by Eric Kim at Harvard's T.H. Chan School of Public Health analyzed how aging, positive thinking, and physical health are linked. In short, his work indicates that having goals, aims, and aspirations that move us forward in life in any form—including a Bucket List—reduces psychological distress and increases health.

This wave of research, writing, and personal development on purpose and aspirations is fundamental to the shift we are living through in American society. Things have changed significantly since 1935, when the retirement age was set at sixty-five. Back then, the average life span for men was sixty-five—today it's seventy-five for men and well into the eighties for women. The fastest-growing category for people starting business is the "post-retirement" age.

What I see is that people without aspirations at whatever age can easily become "stuck" in their lives and caught in a cycle of inward thinking that increases worry and stress. One solution: embrace aspirational thinking, and make it literal using your Bucket List.

Nothing Significant Ever Happens Alone

At this point in the book, it's reasonable to say, "Alright already . . . I wrote my Bucket List. I've got goals for travel, treasures, accomplishments, and experiences." But simply writing it isn't enough. Let's use Jeri Meola's research and her own Bucket List to teach us how three ingredients ensure the highest probability of success:

- A specific "what": drop one-dollar bills off the Empire State Building

- By when: before age sixty-five

- With whom: the person who has agreed to help me

Accountability partners keep plans alive and moving forward. Being specific about "why" and "when" is not enough.

We need a partner to help us tackle the "how."

One item on my Bucket List that I never thought I would complete is skydiving, because I didn't have the "how." When I turned thirty, one of my friends offered to take me . . . and my wife said, "Hell no!" With two little kids and not enough life insurance, she put her foot down and ended that dream pronto. "Maybe when you're fifty," she said with a smirk.

I completely forgot about it.

Imagine my shock when, for my fiftieth birthday, she booked me a skydiving expedition without telling me about it! It was an incredible experience. I didn't have a plan to accomplish that goal, but Melinda knew it was on my list . . . and she was just devilish enough to sit on that

We need a partner to help us tackle the "how."

secret for twenty years. She was my accountability partner, and she filled in the requirements of "by when" and "with whom."

You probably won't complete every item on your Bucket List—I know that I won't. But the only way you'll complete any at all is by deciding not only what but also by when and with whom. Carpe diem, seize the day!

CHAPTER 4:
What We Concentrate on Grows

In 1984, Mark Bergman was meticulously reading Napoleon Hill's *Think and Grow Rich* for the umpteenth time. His wife, Debbie, asked a blunt question only a spouse can ask: "Why do you keep reading that book over and over again? What's the point?"

Mark has the quintessential story of a scrappy, rebellious entrepreneur. He got kicked out of college for shenanigans and was barely allowed back into school. He graduated and was hired to become a financial advisor. But as in college, he was almost immediately restless and rebellious at a desk job. Instead of making money for other people, he wanted to make it for himself. For Mark, *Think and Grow Rich* was a pathway to personal success. "I told Debbie, we're going to start our own business. We both want to make a difference in the world and put ourselves in a financial position to contribute to causes we believe in. That book helped sharpen my aspirations and keep the dream alive."

Mark has always had a strong urge to create, so his aspirational instincts came alive through inventing. The first product was the airplane spoon, a spoon for children that was shaped like an airplane. It was simple and very successful. It worked because parents had been pretending spoons were airplanes for years in attempts to get toddlers to eat . . . but Mark and his business partner at the time, Dan Harris, were the first to actually make a spoon *look* like an airplane. It was a simple stroke of genius, so much so that most people declare, "I should have thought of that!" when they hear this story. But the airplane spoon was only a warm-up for the big leagues.

A few patents later, Mark hit it big with the HANDy Paint Pail. Similar to the airplane spoon, he acted on the instincts most people feel—but Mark drove to make his dream come alive.

"I was painting the trim around our basement in the summer of 2000," he recalls. "There was a lot of trim to paint, and my hand was really tired from holding the paint can—even cramping. So I made a duct-tape strap and attached it to a half-pound Folgers coffee can. It worked! My hand didn't hurt anymore, and the painting got much easier." Eventually, Debbie and their son Christopher both used the prototype tool and agreed, "This is a decent invention. . . . I think you have something here."

While wrestling with patents and fighting off challenges from companies trying to knock off his invention, Mark made his first sale in 2002 to a Midwestern painting store named Hirshfield's. He held firm to a retail price of $9.99, in spite of some major retailers demanding he lower the price. "I knew there was nothing else like this in the industry," Mark explained. He won out. Fifteen years later, average retail is still $9.99, and the HANDy Paint Pail has sold more than 10 million units.

Today, the business is thriving by creating and marketing an entire family of painting products that both professionals and DIYers love. And to make the story even better, two of Mark and Debbie's four children work in the business, as well as his daughter-in-law.

Mark's dream is coming true. How about yours?

Aspirations Create Possibilities

While Mark's story continues to spread throughout the industry, he still points to *Think and Grow Rich* as his guidance for aspirational thinking. In the book, Hill argues that you can't inch your way to success without first believing that success is possible.

Aspirational thinking, huh?

Only once you've celebrated your goal as totally achievable will you spot the small markers of progress along the way.

Aspirational thinking is a simple idea worth repeating. Focusing on goals with positive, hope-based "whys" helps us overcome fear-based decisions that keep us stuck.

Science has proven that positive, aspirational psychology actually causes chemical changes in our bodies and brains. In fact, researchers at McGill University discovered that 72 percent of people with social anxiety showed improvement after just two hours of practicing a simple form of cognitive bias modification: picking a photo of a smiling face out from three other frowning ones. Plus, researchers at the University of Illinois found that businesses with positive, happy workers see performance increase and health insurance costs drop significantly. Aspirational thinking is good for mind, body, and soul.

Only once you've celebrated your goal as totally achievable will you spot the small markers of progress along the way.

Believe It's Possible

Mark and Debbie are poster images for people who are living their Bucket List life. They pictured their success and believed they could live those aspirations. As his friend, and one of the early testers of the HANDy Paint Pail concept, I had no question in my mind that Mark was going to do something significant. He was focused on his aspirations, and he made that vision come alive because he knew that what we concentrate on grows.

So, this begs the questions: What attracts your concentration? Are you concentrating on a never-ending to-do list that has you stuck? Or do you have a compelling Bucket List—one filled with aspirations that will propel you forward?

CHAPTER 5:
Goodness Grows

"Do you believe in your own success or not?"

Mid-2009, that question stopped me in my tracks. Mark Bergman was in my face, challenging me to live my aspirations.

Rewind a bit: I was working in a job that was no longer a good fit for me. The harder I worked, the worse my personal and professional life felt. And on top of that, I was really embarrassed because I was a leadership coach—and I wasn't being an effective leader. I was losing confidence and alienating team members. Worst of all, I was making myself sick with worry and self-doubt.

Here's how Mark helped: I confided in him that running my own leadership consulting firm was on my Bucket List, but I could never bring myself to do it. I was paralyzed by fear—fear of failing in the job I had and fear of failing my family if I ventured out on my own. My fear was worsened by the economic meltdown around us. It was Mark's life-changing question that jarred me loose: *"Do you believe in your own success or not?"*

It was one of those powerful questions that wasn't really a question.

"With a strong vision, failure is not an option," he coached. "You have to stop focusing on the fear and start thinking about living your Bucket List. If you can find a way to visualize a compelling picture of success, you will not fail."

Sometimes Quitting Is Good

Within a year, I was out on my own. It was both scary and thrilling; Melinda and I had two kids in college and a very short window of time to get the business off the ground.

When news spread to clients and friends that I was out on my own, I was inundated with calls for coffee meetings. My voicemail and my inbox were jammed with "thinking of you" notes. It was overwhelming! So at Mark's encouragement, I invited everyone who offered to buy me coffee to get together all at once. I hosted a buy-your-own breakfast event to discuss this question: Where do you see goodness alive and well in the business community today?

Looking back, it was the right idea at the right time. It was during the depths of the Great Recession; people were feeling bruised and confused. My story of focusing on my own picture of success

> *Where do you see goodness alive and well in the business community today?*

turned out to be valuable and inspiring to others. And the conversation about "goodness" was a booster shot of positivity for everyone . . . the room was electric!

So, again with Mark's help, we formalized that buy-your-own breakfast discussion about goodness into the Good Leadership Breakfast Series. The breakfasts are still a signature element of our business today. The enthusiasm around the original breakfast lit the fire of my leadership-coaching firm that I had dreamed of for so many years. I'm no longer sick from stress or embarrassed about my leadership. Today, it feels really good that I quit—because acting on my aspirations got me unstuck and unleashed a whole new life of possibilities.

All I really had to do was allow myself to think freely about how to bring alive the idea that *goodness pays in leadership.* I had to visualize how writing best-selling books, traveling nationally and internationally for speaking engagements, working with my family members in our firm, and starting destination retreats for executives and business owners would be my path. With the support (and pressure) of the people around me, those aspirations have come true. Whether or not the business is growing or the checkbook is overflowing, I am living my Bucket List.

Goodness Multiplies

So, as you might imagine, Mark was one of the first speakers at the Good Leadership Breakfast, and he told the story you read about in Chapter 3.

Before the breakfast, he once again posed a game-changing idea to me. "What if," he ventured, "you ask people to drop donations for charity in a HANDy Paint Pail, and I match whatever donations you raise?" I loved the idea, with one tweak: I suggested we rename the paint pail "The Bucket of Goodwill" to drive home the point.

Since that first morning when we used the bucket like a collection plate, more than 14,000 guests have contributed ones, fives, tens, and occasionally hundreds! In the first six years, we collected and distributed more than $200,000 in donations to charities around the country.

When I took the risk to quit my full-time job, I chased an item on my Bucket List out of hope rather than fear, and the project took on a life of its own. Goodness pays because goodness grows. We have more than $200,000 in charity donations to prove it.

It All Starts with the Seven Fs

The reason I was willing to take the risk was the experimental writing, speaking, and coaching I was doing around a personal leadership concept I developed called the Seven Fs: *faith, family, finances, fitness, friends, fun, and future.* Tim Schmidt and I created the concept to help us be accountable for good leadership—both personally and professionally.

While the recession was crashing around us, the only coaching work I found to be exhilarating and cathartic was probing deeply into the questions surrounding the Seven Fs:

- Faith: How satisfied are you with your spiritual life?

- Family: How satisfied are you with your relationships with loved ones, who share a common sense of home?

- Finances: How satisfied are you with how your money funds your priorities?

- Fitness: How satisfied are you with the health of your body?

- Friends: How satisfied are you with the non-family relationships with people who share your joys and disappointments?

- Fun: How satisfied are you with the part of your life that is playful and joyful?

- Future: How satisfied are you with the hope you have for yourself and others?

Through my own reflections, I realized the risks I perceived in starting my own business were rooted in my own dissatisfaction with "future." Mark called me on it, and he was right. I needed to live my own words. So, I made the leap of faith, investing in "future."

Leading by Example: Sharing My Bucket List

The central idea in Chapter 1 is captivating to me: Instead of making a Bucket List to fulfill the end of your life, why not use the Bucket List to help you live the life you imagine *now*? By sharing my Bucket List here, it's more likely someone will help me fulfill it and equally as likely someone will be inspired.

By virtue of the fact that you're reading this book, I'm living my Bucket List. I am grateful every day for the knowledge that I've accomplished some things that, a few years ago, I thought were a big stretch. Here are some of the things I wrote down on my Bucket List after my intervention with Mark:

- **Write a best-selling book.** Check. *What Really Works: Blending the Seven Fs to Live with Less Stress and Lead with Less Fear* has sold more than 20,000 copies and is still alive today. With the help of my friend Tim Schmidt, I wrote about how building a life around satisfaction in Faith, Family, Finances, Fitness, Friends, Fun, and Future can help build confidence and create good leadership. And I think *The Bucket List Book* is on its way.

- **Golf at St. Andrews for my fiftieth birthday.** Check. I missed it by a year, but that's only because I went skydiving instead of golfing.

- **String our fifty-two-foot pine tree with Christmas lights.** Check. Fifteen years ago, my son Ben asked if we could light the huge tree in our front yard for Christmas. I knew it would be a huge and expensive undertaking. But, on Black Friday 2015 we flipped the switch on six thousand lights to illuminate our Bucket List tree. We were celebrating the success of our family-owned business with more than a hundred people who helped along the way.

- **Own a Paul Granlund sculpture as a memento of my wife Melinda's and my love for our alma mater, Gustavus Adolphus College.** Check. Paul Granlund is one of the most famous American sculptors of the twentieth century, and he attended Gustavus just a couple decades before Melinda and I did. Last year, we bought the artist's copy of my favorite: *Cradle*.

- **Attend the Indianapolis 500**. Check. Perhaps the most appropriate example for this story: Two years after I revealed this item on my Bucket List at one of our coaching retreats, my colleague Kristi Olafson gave me *her*

tickets to the ninety-ninth running of the
Indy 500. She remembered and was delighted
to help!

So now I'm thinking even bigger, and I have my
Grandma Hunter as my mentor. My mother's mother
(whom you learned about in Chapter 3) lived an
adventurous life until the age of 103! Here's how she
influenced me:

A world-class musician, Arlene Urban sang with the
Chicago Opera on the radio in the 1920s, only to return
to rural Iowa under the threat of violence spreading at
the hands of Al Capone's gang. Back in Iowa, Arlene
married Willis Kenneth Hunter, had two daughters, and
spent more than forty-five years teaching music in the
public schools.

As a volunteer, she wrote the hundred-year history
book for her hometown of Lake View, Iowa. For more
than fifty-five years, she read one book per week and
gave each book an "appropriateness rating" for the local
public library.

But it was her musical aspirations that kept her
Bucket List alive until the end. She played the organ in
the church until age ninety-five, when they took her car
keys away for her own safety.

Her most inspiring story involves surviving a triple
bypass open-heart surgery at the age of eighty-nine. The

doctors could not turn away her surgery because her mind was so sharp! During the recovery period, she decided to attempt a feat of musical excellence most college music majors wouldn't tackle. Her goal: to memorize one Chopin étude per month until she finished all twenty-seven. Those who've studied music know an étude is a specific piece of music written to advance the highest level of skill for that instrument. Chopin wrote twenty-seven of these to teach the highest level of piano skill.

My grandmother mastered and memorized all twenty-seven before she turned ninety-three. For her, it was both an accomplishment and an experience tied to her Bucket List. I vividly recall my toddler children sitting next to her on the piano bench while she played some of those études with passion and pride. She may have been playing them slower than was intended, but it was a timeless treasure to anyone who watched and listened.

So, at the age of fifty-three, I'm gazing into my family legacy and thinking: What's my Chopin étude?

Working on a Bucket List is an investment in our future.

Better yet, what's *your* Chopin étude?

You and I might have very different aspirations on our Bucket Lists, but no matter who we are, working on a Bucket List is an investment in our future.

So in the spirit of practicing what I preach, here are some of the aspirational things on my current Bucket List:

- Travel six weeks in Europe with Melinda

- Play golf at Augusta National Golf Course, home of the Masters Tournament

- Take a hot air balloon ride over the Serengeti

- Set foot on all seven continents (three down, four to go . . . even though I have no desire to go to Antarctica)

- Sing a concert with a real gospel choir

- Give away one million dollars to causes I believe in during the second half of my life

- Own a Porsche convertible—even if for one day

- Shoot my age in golf—even if I have to play the kiddie tees when I'm ninety years old

- Write a *New York Times* best-selling book

- Set the Guinness World Record for sending the most thank-you notes from one post office in one day (wouldn't that be a fabulous demonstration of *living generously*?)

I have to admit, it feels weird sharing this list so publicly. I guess I prove the research at the beginning of this book: most Bucket Lists are held in privacy. As I've been writing this chapter, I've been struggling with these questions: Am I feeling self-conscious in sharing this list because I am worried about being perceived as conceited? Am I being self-centered and frivolous? Braggadocious?

Maybe this is why people keep their lists private!

Or maybe I'm feeling vulnerable because, like most people, I sometimes struggle with the idea of asking for help.

One thing is for sure: now that I've shared my Bucket List, I'm more likely to receive help in doing these things. How could anyone help me if I kept my Bucket List a secret?

Reality Check

The point of this chapter is not to convince you to quit your job and start your own business. That's my dream—I don't know your dreams (yet!). My hope is this book creates a "Mark Bergman" moment for you, stopping you in your tracks with the question: *Do you believe in your own success or not?*

CHAPTER 6:

Let's Get Started!

It's time to get to work. No matter how formal or informal your process, working on your Bucket List puts your aspirational thinking on the path to action. Why not make the first item on your Bucket List "make my Bucket List" and share it with someone today?

Here are some ideas to jump-start your thinking:

- Sit down with a friend and challenge one another to identify three things for your Bucket List.

- Read more inspirational authors like Richard Leider and Oprah Winfrey to continue to shape your aspirations.

- Answer the questions on the next page to kick off your brainstorming!

Here are some good questions and resources to get you started on your own list:

- What do you daydream about?

- What daydreams do you share with family members?

- What brought you joy years ago that you want to embrace again?

- What dreams have you ignored or written off out of fear?

- What parts of the world do you want to visit?

- What "toy" would you love to own? A motorcycle? A table loom? A tent? A fancy barbecue grill?

Keep brainstorming, and use the following pages to write down your aspirations for travel, treasures, experiences, and accomplishments.

The following pages are scribble sheets to help you collect and organize your ideas for your Bucket List. Social research for this book surfaced the dreams and aspirations from more than fifty people in the four Bucket List categories:

Travel is about countries, cities, landmarks, or a special place you want to visit.

Treasures is about keepsakes, tools for hobbies, or collections.

Experiences is about adventures that create extra meaning, thrill, or fun.

Accomplishments is about goals or endeavors signified by a commitment over time to achieve.

Examples to stimulate your thinking:

Peter and Elizabeth intend to visit all of the national parks in the United States together.

- Is this Travel, Experience, or Accomplishment? Does it matter?

Jonathan is an avid baseball card collector who wants to acquire a signed Joe DiMaggio rookie card from 1936.

- Is this a Treasure or Accomplishment?

Mike and Kathy are lifelong athletes who are determined to run a marathon in all fifty states.

- Is this Travel, Experience, or Accomplishment?

Travel
Treasures
Experiences
Accomplishments

Ideas for My Bucket List

_____

_____

_____

_____

_____

_____

MY BUCKET LIST

Countries, cities, landmarks, or a special place I want to visit

In the middle of their lives, when they were about to enter into their second marriages to each other, Elizabeth and Peter decided that they needed to have a Bucket List that they shared. They started walking trails in national parks around the country with the intention of visiting every single park. They checked off twelve parks while they were dating, and are working on the other forty-six now that they're married.

Paul and Karen's kids are college-age and older, and to keep the family connected as the kids moved out and away, Peter and Karen started a family travel Bucket List. The rules: each trip must include at least one other family member, and the person who suggests it organizes it.

OTHERS:
Hike the Superior Hiking trail alone
Be baptized in the Nile

Travel suggestions from people like you:

Ride the Trans-Siberian railway and visit Alaska (the only state I haven't visited) —**Erin, 37**

Visits the sites where *The Sound of Music* was filmed —**Robert, 62**

Feel the power and mist of Iguazu Falls, preferably the Argentinian side of the river —**Lisa, 46**

Hike in Nepal, the Swiss Alps, and New Zealand —**Bob, 58**

Visit the countries of my ancestors —**Rita, 57**

Travel my homeland, India, and then go to Egypt and Israel —**Antwel, 33**

Swim in the Mediterranean Sea off the coast of Greece —**Jeremy, 47**

Visit the hot springs in Greenland —**Kate, 52**

Go to Northern Norway at Midsummer, when the sun never sets —**Lorainne, 49**

Take a cruise through the Panama Canal —**Grayson, 37**

Go to Cuba on a jazz music tour —**Chuck, 53**

Visit Ireland for the golf, and Italy for the wine —**Suzanne, 61**

MY TRAVEL IDEAS

Date: _____

What: _____

By When: _____

With Whom: _____

Notes: _____

_____

_____

_____

_____

_____

_____

_____

_____

BUCKET LIST ACTION PLAN

Date: _____

What: _____

By When: _____

With Whom: _____

Notes: _____

_____

_____

_____

_____

_____

_____

_____

_____

BUCKET LIST ACTION PLAN

Date: _____

What: _____

By When: _____

With Whom: _____

Notes: _____

_____

_____

_____

_____

_____

_____

_____

_____

_____

BUCKET LIST ACTION PLAN

Date: _____

What: _____

By When: _____

With Whom: _____

Notes: _____

_____

_____

_____

_____

_____

_____

_____

_____

MY BUCKET LIST

Keepsakes, tools for hobbies, or collections

Jack grew up loving the New York Yankees, and he always dreamed of owning a signed Joe DiMaggio rookie baseball card. At age sixty, he went on a hunt around the country to collectors' conventions, and ultimately bought his treasured baseball card from the family of the original owner. They still exchange Christmas cards!

Jennifer and her husband decided that for the rest of their lives, they will only purchase original art from artists they have met. They've even started replacing existing art in their home, so that ultimately, every piece in their house will have a personal story.

OTHERS:
Have a backyard quail coop
Collect antique typewriters

Treasures suggestions from people like you:

Take a workshop for woodworking like my grandfather and dad
—**Ben, 27**

Become a prolific collector of Beatles memorabilia by anyone's
standards —**Harry, 67**

Collect manual typewriters and antique furniture that capture
my eye —**Eric, 60**

Buy a cello that will last beyond my lifetime —**Hannah, 23**

Build a movie theater in my house with at least twelve seats to
watch movies with my grandkids on the "big screen"
—**Debbie, 61**

Own a Steinway Piano I can pass along for generations in my
family —**Sam, 51**

Buy only original artwork for the rest of my life that will appre-
ciate in financial value —**Terry, 55**

Drive a Mercedes convertible as my main car until I can't drive
anymore —**Dianne, 57**

Acquire one original Matisse painting —**Morgan, 40**

Buy a home in the Bahamas so we can work from there when-
ever I want —**Jim, 55**

MY TREASURES IDEAS

Date: _____

What: _____

By When: _____

With Whom: _____

Notes: _____

_____

_____

_____

_____

_____

_____

_____

_____

_____

BUCKET LIST ACTION PLAN

Date: _____

What: _____

By When: _____

With Whom: _____

Notes: _____

_____

_____

_____

_____

_____

_____

_____

_____

BUCKET LIST ACTION PLAN

Date: _____

What: _____

By When: _____

With Whom: _____

Notes: _____

_____

_____

_____

_____

_____

_____

_____

_____

_____

BUCKET LIST ACTION PLAN

Date: _____

What: _____

By When: _____

With Whom: _____

Notes: _____

_____

_____

_____

_____

_____

_____

_____

_____

MY BUCKET LIST

Adventures which create extra meaning, thrill, or fun

Jason is a fitness instructor, and he and his ten-year-old daughter set a goal to run a triathalon together before she turns eighteen. Their training will start when she's a little older . . . but they're already excited!

Carolyn worked as a backwoods guide in Colorado, and always dreamed of skiing in and out of mountain huts that had been built for military training during World War Two. After a seasonal job ended, she decided it was now or never—so she convinced five friends to try this low-impact version of winter camping, and they skied thirty miles through the Rocky Mountains over five days.

OTHERS:
Take a cooking class in Italy
Summit a mountain

Experiences suggestions from people like you:

Buy an RV in Alaska and drive it all the way home, taking as long as I want, stopping wherever I want —**John, 51**

Celebrate mass in Notre Dame on Christmas Eve
—**Gwen, 58**

Walk at least 100 miles of the Camino De Santiago pilgrimage in Spain —**Mike, 56**

See the Southern Cross from Australia with a full moon
—**Tina, 46**

Be re-baptized in the Nile —**Anonymous**

Be a back-up singer in a band —**PK, 47**

Hike the Superior Hiking Trail by myself —**Laura, 30**

Go on a week-long silent retreat —**Twanya, 43**

Take an Italian cooking class in Italy —**Karen, 50**

Conduct a bona fide orchestra rehearsal for one hour
—**David, 53**

MY EXPERIENCES IDEAS

Date: _____

What: _____

By When: _____

With Whom: _____

Notes: _____

_____

_____

_____

_____

_____

_____

_____

_____

_____

BUCKET LIST ACTION PLAN

Date: _____

What: _____

By When: _____

With Whom: _____

Notes: _____

_____

_____

_____

_____

_____

_____

_____

_____

BUCKET LIST ACTION PLAN

Date: _____

What: _____

By When: _____

With Whom: _____

Notes: _____

_____

_____

_____

_____

_____

_____

_____

_____

_____

BUCKET LIST ACTION PLAN

Date: _____

What: _____

By When: _____

With Whom: _____

Notes: _____

_____

_____

_____

_____

_____

_____

_____

_____

MY BUCKET LIST

Goals or endeavors signified by a commitment over time to achieve

Rick, the elderly caretaker at a senior living complex, discovered that one of the residents taught voice lessons. Rick was raised in a family where the men were expected not to make music, but he had always dreamed of singing in public—so he asked the resident to teach him. After three and a half years of voice lessons, he led Christmas carols at the senior center and sang "O Holy Night" as a solo.

When George and Jake got married, they joined their shared love of raising dahlias. Their dream was to win a blue ribbon at their state fair—not only did they win one, they won eighteen in a single year!

OTHERS:
Start my own cooking show
Flip a house

Accomplishments suggestions from people like you:

Successfully flip a house and actually make some money in the process —**Debbie, 58**

Start my own backcountry cooking show —**Reily, 26**

Appear in court and try a winning court case for a survivor of domestic violence —**Alina, 26**

Start my own business and successfully pass it down to my children —**Enrico, 44**

Be the first person in my family to graduate from college —**Amahn, 22**

Have a building named after me at the college where I got my first degree —**Dan, 59**

Belong to Pine Valley Country Club —**Scott, 48**

Buy at least 33 percent of a vineyard in California or Oregon —**Doug, 51**

Write a piece of choral music that gets published and sold —**Katrina, 36**

Complete one of the 12 Epic Mud Run Races before I turn 50 —**Artie, 46**

ACCOMPLISHMENTS

MY ACCOMPLISHMENTS IDEAS

Date: _____

What: _____

By When: _____

With Whom: _____

Notes: _____

_____

_____

_____

_____

_____

_____

_____

_____

BUCKET LIST ACTION PLAN

Date: _____

What: _____

By When: _____

With Whom: _____

Notes: _____

_____

_____

_____

_____

_____

_____

_____

_____

ACCOMPLISHMENTS

BUCKET LIST ACTION PLAN

Date: _____

What: _____

By When: _____

With Whom: _____

Notes: _____

_____

_____

_____

_____

_____

_____

_____

_____

_____

BUCKET LIST ACTION PLAN

Date: _____

What: _____

By When: _____

With Whom: _____

Notes: _____

_____

_____

_____

_____

_____

_____

_____

_____

Additional Resources for Building YOUR Bucket List

- Richard Leider's work with AARP on regaining purpose: lifereimagined.aarp.org/ OR lifereimagined.aarp.org/ expert/17801-richard-leider

- Where on this list would you love to go? travel.usnews.com/Rankings/ Worlds_Best_Vacations/

- Visit this web site: makeavisionboard.com to spark your aspirational thinking.

CHAPTER 7:

What Does a Bucket List Have to Do with Good Leadership?

It's a reasonable question: What does a Bucket List have to do with good leadership? But the better question is: *Why should someone follow you?*

Ever heard the phrases "There goes a woman on a mission" or "That guy is going places"? These are expressions to describe leaders with vivid aspirations. Followers find aspirational leaders to be magnetic.

The opposite of an aspirational leader is someone who is "stuck." Who wants to give a full mind, body, and soul commitment to follow someone who is stuck? The Bucket List is an excellent exercise to stimulate aspirational thinking to create positive momentum when leaders are stuck.

Aspirational Thinking at Work

Scholar and business authority Jim Collins coined the phrase "Big Hairy Audacious Goal" in his block-buster book *Built to Last*. His research concluded that organizations that endured the test of time were pro-pelled forward by an audacious goal—something that could only be accomplished a minimum of twenty years into the future. The word "hairy" makes the concept vis-ceral; it makes a goal feel real. But "hairy" also describes the emotional part of an audacious goal: If the goal is bold enough, it will cause the hair on your arms to tin-gle. Big. Hairy. Audacious. Goal.

Big, hairy, audacious goals (BHAGs) are part of what makes growing an organization so exciting . . . and BHAGs are also what make a Bucket List so exciting.

At age fifty-three, I'm still counting on *two* twenty-year time horizons for my Bucket List. Remember, my grandmother lived to be 103.

From the first day we started our leadership coach-ing firm, our coaches have been using aspirational and Bucket List thinking to stimulate positive momentum for leaders. And it works! Hundreds of clients know that creating an actual Bucket List will provide a tool for accountability and action to improve their lives and their leadership.

A Living Example: Aspirations at Work

Jodi Harpstead is someone who sparked the power of Bucket List–style thinking for me in the workplace. She's an accomplished CEO whose personal and professional life is a magic carpet ride.

She played a critical role in the meteoric growth of the medical device company Medtronic. Over more than twenty years with Medtronic, she was offered a much-larger-than-normal variety of leadership roles. It was a world-class development opportunity that helped fuel her aspirations for today.

Jodi reflects, "What I discovered through a company-sponsored training at GAP International was life altering for me. My coach taught me an aspirational thinking concept called Breakthrough Thinking. A breakthrough goal is a goal that I *barely believe is possible* and *don't know how to achieve*, but would be a huge breakthrough for me personally and professionally."

One year, Jodi invested the time and energy to ensure that everyone in her sales organization had formulated a clear and compelling aspirational breakthrough goal. "That year we blew our sales goals away by forty percent over expectations. And I've been using the concept in my leadership ever since," Jodi says.

Today, Jodi is the CEO of Lutheran Social Service of Minnesota, and she's cascading the aspirational concept of breakthrough goals through the organization.

Aspirational thinking is not just about dreaming big; it's about articulating what success looks like—and by when—in front of your peers.

"We don't pass judgment. We create an aspirational culture where leaders are encouraged to work toward something extraordinary. Even if we don't get to the breakthrough, we create many new and wonderful results that otherwise would not have happened."

Isn't that the same concept as your Bucket List? What harm is there in declaring to your family and friends: "I want to set foot on every continent, and I need your help!" The discussion, planning, and research on social media and travel sites will make life more exciting. And your mood will be more positive whether or not you actually set foot on Antartica.

The Aspirational Formula for Good Leadership: 20-7-3-1

Good leaders learn to communicate the aspirational thinking process in a sequence of 20-7-3-1 years to help stimulate aspiration in a realistic and motivating framework.

20 Years Ahead: *Your BHAG*

Jim Collins articulates a twenty-year aspirational framework with his BHAG. What is your Big. Hairy. Audacious. Goal? The BHAG is a powerful tool to help leaders consider their mission and purpose for a good life.

7 Years Ahead: *Your Personal Vision*

Seven years is the most effective timeframe for *personal visioning.* Aspirational leaders ask themselves, "What will my life look like, by when?" The "what" is motivated by the "by when." Think of it as your own personal version of Jodi Harpstead's Breakthrough Thinking.

The seven-year personal visioning aligns very closely with the timeframe most people use for their Bucket List.

3 Years Ahead: *Your Personal and Professional Strategic Plan*

A three-year planning window helps you identify milestones over the next three years to make your seven-year vision come alive.

1 Year Ahead: *Your Satisfaction Today on the Seven Fs*

Finally, the "1" in the 20-7-3-1 aspirational framework is all about the here and now. It's about making an intellectually honest assessment of the things that really count in life today: your satisfaction with your faith, family, finances, fitness, friends, fun, and future . . . the Seven Fs! The literal connection to the Bucket List concept is that last F—future.

Choose the number between 1 and 10 that describes your own satisfaction with each of the Seven Fs.

	Low				Medium					High
Faith	My spiritual life									
	1	2	3	4	5	6	7	8	9	10
Family	My loved ones, who share a common sense of "home"									
	1	2	3	4	5	6	7	8	9	10
Finances	How money funds the priorities in my life									
	1	2	3	4	5	6	7	8	9	10
Fitness	The strength and health of my body									
	1	2	3	4	5	6	7	8	9	10
Friends	People who know me well and support my joys, disappointments, and dreams									
	1	2	3	4	5	6	7	8	9	10
Fun	The part of my life that is playful and joyful									
	1	2	3	4	5	6	7	8	9	10
Future	The hope we have for ourselves and for others									
	1	2	3	4	5	6	7	8	9	10

Finding Your Momentum

Let's transfer your satisfaction scores from pages 90–91 onto the Seven Fs Wheel.

A well-tuned Seven Fs wheel generates positive momentum in both our personal and professional lives.

Instructions:

Circle the number between 1 (low) and 10 (high) that indicates your current satisfaction on each of The Seven Fs on the wheel. Then, starting with the highest number, connect the dots.

Here's the Seven Fs Wheel for you to assess the Seven Fs in your life:

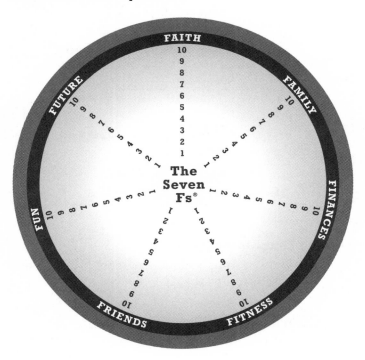

How does your satisfaction with the Seven Fs affect your ability for aspirational thinking?

Aspirational thinking is the fuel for innovation.
Aspirational thinking sparks healthy tension.
Aspirational thinking stimulates growth.
Aspirational thinking motivates people to work toward higher performance, both personally and professionally.

The only way to get to the twenty-year framework is to start your aspirational thinking *right now*.

It works for Mark Bergman. It works for Jodi Harpstead. It worked for my grandmother. I believe it's working for me. Why not you?

Here's the Aspirational Leadership Framework at a glance:

20 Years Ahead—*your BHAG*

7 Years Ahead—*your personal vision*

3 Years Ahead—*your personal and professional strategic plan*

1 Year Ahead—*your Seven Fs in the current year*

Carpe diem.

Find help for improving your leadership by getting *The Bright Paper: How Breakthrough Aspirational Thinking Sparks Growth in You and Your Enterprise* at GoodLeadership.com

CHAPTER 8

The Bucket List Game

You've probably played plenty of icebreakers and team-building exercises. Why not try the Bucket List Game?

Years ago, we developed a little game for dinner parties and team-building events. We wanted something that could bring people together in a meaningful way . . . something that could really go *deeper* than just talking about kids' sports teams and television shows we binge-watched on Netflix.

Here's your chance to play the Bucket List Game.

The rules are easy: Players guess which Bucket List items belong to whom, and the owner of each list shares the "Why?" behind his or her aspirations with the group. The Bucket List Game can be used in three contexts:

- **To enhance friendships:** In a situation like a dinner party, guessing each other's goals is exciting, and explaining your own goals to your friends is even better.

- **To strengthen relationships on an existing team:** In the daily grind, it's too common that teammates barely get past "How was your weekend?" much less asking each other's hopes and dreams. Increasing this relational component strengthens teamwork.

- **To jump-start new relationships:** We've all done a thousand icebreakers, but asking someone's favorite television show hardly strengthens new relationships. Sharing quirky, interesting aspirations is a fun, honest interaction that new teammates will never forget.

Some people are hesitant to share their Bucket Lists. That's the beauty of the Bucket List Game. Players aren't required to share their deepest yearnings, just three items. It's fun! The best part:

I have personally witnessed dozens of times when a player says their goal out loud, and another player replies, **"Hey, I can help you with that."**
—Paul Batz

Let's play!

Rules

Players sit or stand in a configuration where all players can see and hear one another. The facilitator will identify the person whose birthday is nearest to today as the person who begins the game. That person is the "Guesser."

1. The facilitator will read one Bucket List Participation Sheet and ask "the Guesser" to identify which player best matches the three items mentioned.

2. If your name is called upon and the three items are not yours, then you are the Guesser and you must guess who best matches the three items. This sequence continues until the person is successfully identified.

3. When the person is identified successfully, then the person explains the three items, and he/she is now the new "Guesser."

4. In groups of twelve or more, after seven unsuccessful guesses, the facilitator will ask "Whose Bucket List is this?" and the person will reveal themselves. That person is now the Guesser for the next round.

5. The game continues until the last person has been matched with his/her items.

Bucket List Game

Inspired by the 2007 film *The Bucket List*, the purpose of the Bucket List Game is to stimulate aspirational thinking about "What's Possible?" in your life—and to encourage you to share three items from your Bucket List with others who may be able to help.

Write **three items** from your Bucket List in the space provided below, then hand this sheet to the facilitator of the Bucket List Game. DO NOT WRITE YOUR NAME ON THIS PARTICIPATION SHEET.

1. _____

2. _____

3. _____

Bucket List Game

Inspired by the 2007 film *The Bucket List*, the purpose of the Bucket List Game is to stimulate aspirational thinking about "What's Possible?" in your life–and to encourage you to share three items from your Bucket List with others who may be able to help.

Write **three items** from your Bucket List in the space provided below, then hand this sheet to the facilitator of the Bucket List Game. DO NOT WRITE YOUR NAME ON THIS PARTICIPATION SHEET.

1. _____

2. _____

3. _____